BUSINESS CREDIT MASTER MANUAL

A Step-by-step guide to obtaining over $100k in funding for your business.

LEE PRICE III

Copyright Page

Business Credit Master Manual: A Step-by-Step Guide to Getting Over $100,000 in Funding for Your Business

Table of Contents

Business Credit Master Manual

The world of business credit can **seem** overwhelming and complex. In the *Business Credit Master Manual*, I simplify the process of building business credit **through clear, practical steps**. This guide takes you from **launching** your first company to securing **more than $100,000** in business funding.

Whether **you are** an experienced entrepreneur or just getting started, this book provides a **straightforward** roadmap to Success. You'll **discover how to build and expand your** business credit without relying on your personal credit **history**. Each step is **clearly explained, allowing you to take immediate action.**

Access to funding can often determine whether your business thrives or struggles. The Business Credit Master Manual is a practical, results-driven guide designed to help you get funded and achieve long-term financial Success. Let's use business credit to **bring your vision to life!**

PREFACE

Lee Price III is a proud father, Chairman, and CEO of several successful companies. His business interests span real estate, logistics, entertainment, and Private Equity. Born in Oklahoma City, Oklahoma, and raised in Houston, Texas, Mr. Price has grown from small-town beginnings into big-business Success.

At just **sixteen** years old, he began attending Texas Southern University, where he quickly realized that college alone wouldn't teach him how to build wealth. Determined to take control of his future, he launched his first business, an event promotion company called Price Iz Rite Entertainment, **where** he mastered sales and marketing, **honing** the skills that would serve him for the rest of his life.

Success, **however, did not come without setbacks.** Like many young entrepreneurs, Price made some poor decisions and became involved with the wrong people, which led to his incarceration. Although **he isn't proud of this period, he considers it a defining turning point in his life.** During his imprisonment, he devoted himself to studying business, finance, real estate, and personal development. His personal motto became: "He turned Jail into Yale."

This period ignited his passion for teaching and motivating others. He began mentoring fellow inmates, many of whom had also made mistakes but possessed untapped potential. He taught them business, **Self-improvement,** and even GED courses, preparing them to reenter society with new skills and confidence.

After his release, Price shifted his complete focus to real estate. With **limited funds, he began wholesaling properties, finding** deals, securing contracts, and assigning them to investors for profit. His creativity and persistence paid off.

He later launched Price Iz Rite Logistics LLC, a trucking company, starting with a single Ford F-350 and a 40-foot flatbed trailer. Through determination and vision, he grew it into a full-service trucking operation serving both the U.S. and Canada.

Although he achieved great Success in logistics, Price's true passion remained real estate. He transitioned into commercial real estate, focusing on multifamily properties. Over time, his deals have grown larger, and he has been involved in over $500 million in real estate transactions, spanning brokerage, development, acquisitions, and financing.

Beyond his roles as Chairman and CEO, Price is passionate about writing and inspiring others. His mission is to prove that anyone, regardless of background or past mistakes, can achieve Success. Of all his accomplishments, he considers his greatest to be his son, Lee Price IV, as well as his continued philanthropic work.

INTRODUCTION

First, I would like to thank you for selecting the Business Credit Master Manual. I know there are countless books out there, but, as I've learned, time **is our most valuable asset**. It's the one thing we can never get back, so thank you again for taking the time to read this book.

I wrote this manual to show you how to build business credit and secure funding. Over the years, I've read numerous books on business credit, and most of them tend to sugarcoat the truth. They paint a pretty picture but **fail to provide** the real steps to make it happen. In this book, I cut out the fluff and get straight to the point with practical information.

You'll also learn how to limit exposure and protect your privacy. Maybe you've made mistakes in life, or **perhaps** you **simply prefer** to operate more privately. Whether you're starting your first business or you already own **a business that needs funding to grow, this book is for you.**

I need you to adopt **a long-term mindset.** Everything great in life takes time to develop. Even you took nine months to develop before you were born. Building a business, establishing business credit, and becoming a successful CEO **take** patience, effort, and consistency.

I've met countless people who **have asked** me the same question: "How do I get funding to start my business?" If that's your question too, this book just might be the answer you've been searching for.

Ladies and gentlemen, this book **will guide you** to the money. I will show you, step by step, how to build and utilize your business credit. This isn't some "get-rich-quick" scheme or fast-money scam. I cannot stress this enough: this process will take time, patience, and some upfront capital. But trust me, it can be done.

Let's be real: you're crazy if you want to start a business but don't want it to be financially successful. Everyone wants freedom, the freedom that money provides. You want to **travel, spend time with your family, and live without money being a constant obstacle.** If you want financial freedom, then you are in the right place.

There is never a "perfect" time to start a business. The time is **now.** It doesn't matter how old or young you are. Starting a business gives you freedom, and there's no limit to how **far** it can grow. Who knows? Your business could be the next trillion-dollar company.

It all starts in your mind. You must be able to think it, see it, and believe it even when no one else does. Think of an asthmatic gasping for air; they don't care about politics, social media, or parties. Their only focus is oxygen. That's precisely how badly you must want **Success.** I don't care if you've been to prison, gone through a divorce, been abused, or felt unloved. None of that matters now. What matters is creating generational wealth for your family and for yourself.

Owning a business isn't easy. You will face challenges, setbacks, and failures. But you will always get out what you put in. Many people give up too soon, but if you keep pushing forward, Success will come.

Another misconception I often hear is: "I want a business so I don't have a boss." That's the wrong mindset. In business, you actually have two bosses: your customers and your employees. Both of them can fire you and put you out of business if you don't take care of them.

The truth is, business is a lifelong learning process. You must be serious about your growth. Education, technology, and AI are changing the way we do business. If you're not constantly learning and adapting, you will be left behind.

Now, let's do a quick exercise. Take a sheet of paper and draw a line down the middle. On the left side, write down all your goals. On the right side, list the names of everyone you have communicated with in the past week, whether via email, text, calls, or social media. Everything. Now, cross off the names that have nothing to do with your goals.

You'll be surprised at how many people are wasting your time. The people you surround yourself with either push you forward or hold you back. Show me your friends, and I'll show you your net worth.

If you spend time with broke people, chances are you'll end up broke. Surround yourself with people who are ahead of you, people you can learn from, and people who inspire you to grow. Eagles don't fly with pigeons.

One of the hardest lessons I learned was letting go of toxic people, places, and habits, even if they were friends or family. Not everyone is meant to go with you to the next level. Love some people from a distance, but stay focused on your vision. This journey requires discipline, and you can't afford to waste time.

Some of us were taught that "money isn't everything." While that may sound good, the reality is **that** money is a tool, and we need it to survive and to help others. Money gives you the ability to care for your family, **support causes, and make an impact on the world.** Without money, your options are limited. So, never feel guilty about chasing financial freedom.

You must also learn to hustle for your last name, not your first name. Build something that outlives you. **Think of** names like Rockefeller, Carnegie, Morgan, Vanderbilt, and Ford. Their families continue to benefit today from businesses started over a century ago.

At first, you'll wear every hat in your business: CEO, CFO, marketer, salesperson, even janitor. However, your long-term goal is to build a machine that can operate with or without human intervention. Create a team, delegate, and scale. That's how you build generational wealth.

After you're gone, what will your family have to live on? I want you to plan so far ahead that your legacy lasts beyond your lifetime. Personally, I've set a goal for my estate to earn $500 million **annually** for my family by 2095. You may have a different number, but the principle is the same: if you don't plan, you plan to fail.

Life will throw obstacles at you, but you must adapt, adjust, and keep moving forward. Knowledge alone isn't power; applied knowledge is power. Use what you learn in this book and put it into action.

Purchasing this book **is** one of the best investments you could make for your future. Now, let's get started building your business credit and securing the funding to grow your empire.

Hopefully, I'll see you at the top.

Much Success,

Lee Price III

IG: @PriceIzRite

YouTube: @LeePriceIII

TikTok: @LeePriceIII

Facebook: Lee Price III

CHAPTER 1

BUSINESS FORMATIONS

We have two ears and one mouth so that we can listen twice as much as we speak."

— Epictetus

There are several different ways to start a business. In the business world, these are referred to as entity formations. So let's jump right into the other entity formations you can use to get your business started.

Doing Business As (A.K.A. DBA)

A lot of you may already be familiar with this one. It's very common to hear about DBAs when you're new to starting a business. To set up a DBA, you typically visit your local District Clerk's Office website and file the document. This usually costs between $10 and $25.

Now here's my advice: don't start your business with a DBA.

I call it **"the poor man's way"** of doing business. A DBA is usually in your personal name and only puts the public on notice that you're "doing business as" whatever name you file.

For example, if James Smith files for a DBA, he will now be "James Smith d/b/a Smith Trucking." The problem? If Smith Trucking ever gets sued, James Smith himself is on the hook. There's no protection **because the business and owner are legally** the same. That's a considerable risk.

And when it comes to building business credit, banks and creditors do not take DBAs seriously. If you're serious about **establishing** a business and securing funding, consider skipping the DBA.

Pro Tip: A DBA is fine if you just need a side hustle name (like "Jane's Cleaning Service"), but don't rely on it for serious business or credit building

Corporations

A corporation is a more advanced type of business entity. Whenever you see "Inc." after a company name, it indicates that the company is incorporated.

To **form** a corporation, you **must** file the **required** paperwork with **your** state's Secretary of State. Many big companies incorporate in Delaware because the state offers certain legal and tax benefits.

But let me keep it real with you: corporations can be complicated. They require annual meetings, recorded minutes, and strict adherence to corporate laws, even if you're the sole owner.

Corporations also come with two main tax structures: C-Corp and S-Corp. (LLCs can also elect these tax structures.)

C-Corp

- C-Corps pay both federal and state taxes.

- Profits are taxed twice, once at the corporate level and again when shareholders/owners pay personal taxes on dividends.

That's proper double taxation. The company pays taxes, and then you, as the owner, pay again on your share of the profits.

This setup

Pro Tip: If your dream is to secure venture capital funding or go public one day, consider forming a Delaware C-Corp. However, if your goal is to secure financing through business credit, an LLC is a more straightforward option.

S-Corp

- S-Corps do not pay federal or state taxes directly.
- Profits "pass through" and are taxed only once on the owner's individual tax returns.

To elect S-Corp status, you must file IRS Form 2553. If you decide to go this route, consult a CPA or attorney **to avoid mistakes.** Many companies can help file your incorporation paperwork, but always do your research.

Pro Tip: You can start an LLC and later elect S-Corp status for tax purposes. This provides flexibility without the upfront headaches associated with a corporation.

Limited Liability Company (A.K.A. LLC)

In my opinion, the LLC is one of the best business structures ever created. An LLC gives you limited liability protection, meaning the business is separate from you personally.

This separation is **often referred to as the corporate veil.** If the business is sued, your personal assets are typically protected from being used to settle the lawsuit. (The exception: if you mix business with personal use, amongst other things, a court could "pierce the veil." Don't do that.)

An LLC can do almost everything:

- Enter contracts
- Lease or purchase property
- Buy vehicles
- Open bank accounts
- Obtain financing and credit cards

Unlike corporations, LLCs don't require annual meetings or recorded minutes. You should still keep records, but you're not legally required to.

You form an LLC by filing paperwork with your state's Secretary of State. The process is relatively simple, but laws vary by state.

Best States to Form an LLC

You can form an LLC in any state, but not all states are equal. Some, like Texas, require the owners' names to be listed on public documents, meaning anyone can look up your information.

Other states, such as Nevada, Delaware, and my personal favorite, Wyoming, offer stronger privacy protections. In Wyoming, you are not required to list the owners on the formation documents. An authorized representative can handle the filing on your behalf.

I recommend Wyoming if you want maximum privacy. You can live anywhere in the U.S. and still form a Wyoming LLC.

One excellent option is WyomingLLCAttorney.com. For about $200, they will:

- File all necessary paperwork
- Provide a registered agent
- Give your LLC a Wyoming address
- Keep your personal information private

That $200 **fee covers** your first year. **Afterward, the annual renewal** fee is about $169. For privacy and convenience, it's worth it.

Pro Tip: Wyoming is an excellent jurisdiction for holding companies and maintaining privacy. However, if you plan to physically operate in another state (such as opening a storefront in Texas), you may also need to register as a "foreign LLC" (LLC) in that state.

Registered Agent

A registered agent is a person or company that receives legal documents on behalf of your LLC. Every state requires one.

Do not **act as your** own registered agent. It **can be stressful and may compromise** your privacy. Most professional services charge between $35 and $150 per year.

The Wyoming service I mentioned earlier includes a registered agent as part of its package. They'll also provide you with a business address, which is another layer of protection for your privacy.

Operating Agreement

An operating agreement is a legal document that outlines the operational structure of your LLC. It covers things like:

- Who the owners are and their contributions
- How profits are split
- Who can open bank accounts or take out loans
- How taxes are handled

Although it's not required by law, I **strongly** recommend having one. Banks will often request it before allowing you to open an account or obtain financing.

You can create your own operating agreement, buy a template online, or use the attorney service I mentioned earlier.

Pro Tip: Even if you're a one-person LLC, it's still a good idea to create an operating agreement. It makes you look professional and keeps your business credit file clean.

Naming Your LLC

This is the fun part, picking a name for your business.

Here's the truth: your **business name** doesn't matter until you make it matter. Steve Jobs was once ridiculed for naming his company Apple. Look at Apple now.

That said, if privacy is a concern, consider avoiding using your personal name in the company name. For example, avoid naming your business "Jay Smith Trucking LLC" if you want to maintain privacy.

You should also avoid overly industry-specific names. Banks and lenders sometimes see that as a risk factor.

Before finalizing a name, make sure it's available by doing the following:

- Search Google
- Check your state's Secretary of State website
- Use services like Knowx.com for nationwide searches

Pro Tip: Banks use NAICS industry codes to classify businesses. If you're in a "high-risk" category like trucking, finance, or real estate investing, you may face stricter lending rules. A broad, flexible name gives you more options.

Final Thoughts on LLCs

You don't need to live in Wyoming to form a Wyoming LLC. You can live in Ohio, Texas, or anywhere else and still benefit from Wyoming's privacy laws.

If you plan to **do business** in your home state, you may need to file a "foreign entity" notice with your Secretary of State. But if you're just building credit for now, you can skip that step.

If you haven't formed your LLC yet, do it now. Don't procrastinate. Invest the $200, file the paperwork, and make it official. Within a few days, you'll receive your Certificate of Formation and Articles of Organization. That means you are officially in business.

CHAPTER 2

BUSINESS PROFILE SETUP

"The difference between taking a calculated risk and simply rolling the dice can be expressed in one word: homework."

— Georgette Mosbacher

Now that you have your LLC and EIN, it's time to make your business appear official. This is where many people go wrong. Being new doesn't mean you have to *look* new.

When lenders, vendors, or clients look you up, you want to look like you've been in business for years. First impressions matter. They can determine whether you're approved or denied for funding.

I learned this lesson early when I launched my trucking company. I only had one truck and one trailer. Still, because I invested in a solid website and ensured I presented myself professionally online, people assumed my company was larger than it actually was. That Credibility gave me a head start with lenders and clients.

Let's make your business look like it's worth a million dollars from day one.

Step 1: Get a Domain Name & Website

Your domain name (yourbusiness.com) is your online real estate. It should be simple, professional, and as close to your business name as possible.

Use providers like Namecheap, Google Domains, or GoDaddy to buy your domain (usually $10–$20 per year).

Always add domain privacy protection to keep your personal information private online.

Once you have your domain, you need a website.

A website is no longer optional. Lenders and creditors often verify this information before approving funding. Your website should clearly show:

1. Who are you

2. What you do

3. How clients or vendors can contact you

Pro Tip: You don't have to spend thousands on a website. Platforms like Wix, Squarespace, and WordPress make it easy to build a professional site for under $200. Or you can hire freelancers on Fiverr or Upwork to design one for $100–$500. With AI, everything is changing.

Step 2: Create a Professional Email

The first step is setting up a business email. Avoid using Gmail, Yahoo, or Hotmail addresses, as lenders and vendors often view these as red flags.

Your business email should match your domain name (example: info@YourBusinessName.com).

Pro Tip (2025 update): Instead of GoDaddy for email, I recommend Google Workspace or Microsoft 365 Business. Both cost about $6–$12 per month, and they give you:

A professional domain-based email

Cloud storage

Shared calendars

Business tools you'll need anyway

This one small step can instantly boost your Credibility.

Step 3: Virtual Office Address

Never use your home address for business purposes. It appears unprofessional and may lead to your applications being denied. If you can't lease a physical office, use a virtual office address. Companies like Regus, Opus Virtual Offices, and Alliance Virtual Offices provide you with:

A professional business address

Mail handling and forwarding

Optional receptionist/phone services

These usually cost $50–$150 per month. Compared to leasing an office for thousands, this is a more brilliant move when you're just starting.

Pro Tip: Ensure *the virtual office you* select is located in a legitimate commercial building, not a P.O. Box or a UPS Store. *Banks will reject P.O. Boxes and "Suite #123 at the Post Office."*

Step 4: Business Phone Number

Avoid using your personal cell phone as your business line. Lenders and vendors check for a separate business phone number.

Options: Google Voice (free, but not as strong for Credibility)

Grasshopper, RingCentral, or Vonage (VOIP business phone systems)

A business line through AT&T, Verizon, or T-Mobile Business

Register the number in your business name and keep it consistent across all your accounts.

Pro Tip: *When you establish business credit, consider switching to a business mobile account. It not only looks more legitimate but can also appear as a tradeline on your business credit report.*

Step 5: Business Logo & Branding

Your logo is usually the first thing people notice. Please keep it simple, clean, and professional.

Hire a designer on Fiverr or Canva Pro ($20–$100). Use consistent colors, fonts, and style across your website, social media, and business cards

Remember, your logo represents your brand in the long term. It will appear on your website, contracts, and possibly the side of your future office or truck.

Step 6: Business Presence Everywhere

Once you have your domain, email, phone number, and office address, ensure they're consistent everywhere. That means:

Secretary of State filing

IRS records

Bank accounts

Website

Google Business Profile

Business directories

Pro Tip: *Inconsistent business information is the number one reason credit applications are rejected. Lenders check databases, and if your address is listed differently in one place, it can throw up red flags.*

Final Thoughts on Your Business Profile

This is the foundation of your Credibility. Before applying for funding, ensure that lenders, vendors, and partners view a professional business that appears well-established and reliable.

- LLC
- EIN
- Business email
- Website
- Virtual office
- Phone line
- Logo
- Consistency everywhere

Now you're ready to start moving into the world of business banking and credit applications with confidence.

CHAPTER 3

EMPLOYER IDENTIFICATION NUMBER (EIN)

"Don't wait. The time will never be right."

— Napoleon Hill

You **may have heard the term** *EIN* **before.** Some people refer to it as a Federal Tax ID Number. An EIN, which stands for Employer Identification Number, is **essentially** the Social Security number for your business.

Your EIN identifies your company with the government, IRS, banks, and credit bureaus. It's completely separate from your personal Social Security number. That separation gives you the **ability** to build business credit that **doesn't depend** on your individual credit.

Here are a few things you'll use your EIN for:

- Filing tax returns
- Opening business bank accounts
- Applying for business credit cards
- Applying for loans
- Leasing or purchasing vehicles or property
- Building business credit profiles with the major credit bureaus

Pro Tip: *If you don't have an EIN, your business is not considered "real" in the eyes of banks and lenders.* **Obtaining one is the first**

step in separating yourself from your hustle and becoming a legitimate business.

How to Apply for an EIN:

Obtaining an EIN is a simple, free process that can be completed online in under 15 minutes.

Go to www.IRS.gov and find the "Apply for an EIN" section.

The online application is available **Monday to Friday, 7 a.m. to 10 p.m. EST** (the IRS extended these hours a few years ago).

Here's a step-by-step walkthrough:

- Step 1. Click Apply Online Now.
- Step 2. Select your business structure (LLC, Corporation, etc.).
- Step 3. Enter how many members (owners) your LLC has, and select your state.
- Step 4. Select "Start a New Business."
- Step 5. Enter the "Responsible Party" (typically you, the individual owner).
- Step 6. Enter your personal information.
- Step 7. Enter the address of your business/LLC.
- Step 8. Provide details about your business.
- Step 9. Answer if your business owns or operates vehicles with a gross weight of 50,000 lbs. (Most new businesses will answer No here unless you're in trucking.)
- Step 10. Select your industry/business type from the options provided.
- Step 11. Choose how you'd like to receive your EIN confirmation letter. Select online for instant access.

When you're done, the IRS will immediately generate your EIN Confirmation Letter (Form CP 575). **Download, print, and store it safely in multiple places.** Banks and lenders will frequently request this.

Pro Tip: *The EIN application is free of charge.* ***Avoid companies that charge $75–$300 to "get your EIN for you."*** *Go directly to the IRS website.*

Why the EIN is So Important

An EIN does more than register your business with the IRS. It's the foundation of your business credit identity.

Every time you open a bank account, apply for a loan, or request a credit card under your business name, lenders use your EIN to track your history. Over time, this builds your business credit profile with agencies like Dun & Bradstreet, Experian Business, and Equifax Business.

Pro Tip: *Use your EIN instead of your Social Security number* **whenever possible.** *This keeps your business separate from your personal credit, lowers risk to your personal score, and helps your company stand on its own.*

Congratulations – You're Official

Once you've received your EIN, you've taken a significant step in turning your hustle into a real business. Keep your EIN confirmation letter in a safe place. You'll need it **often** for:

- Opening accounts
- Applying for credit
- Verifying your business with vendors and lenders

With your EIN in place, you're now positioned to open business bank accounts and begin building your company's credit profile.

CHAPTER 4

LISTING BUSINESS INFORMATION ONLINE

"Empty pockets never held anyone back. Only empty heads and empty hearts can do that."

— Norman Vincent Peale

This step can make or break your business credit journey. When lenders and vendors review your application, the first thing they do is look you up online. If they can't find you or worse, if your information doesn't match across platforms, they may immediately reject your application.

I cannot stress this enough: your business information must remain consistent across all platforms. Your business name, address, phone number, website, and email address must be consistent and accurate across all directories and listings. A single typo, outdated address, or mismatched phone number can lead to denial.

Think of this process as building your digital footprint. You want to look credible and professional the very first time someone searches your business online.

Step 1: Core Listings You Must Have

Google Business Profile (formerly Google My Business)

Go to business.google.com

Enter your full business details (name, address, phone, website, hours, logo).

Google will send a verification code to the business address associated with your account. A virtual office is acceptable, but avoid using a P.O. Box. Once verified, you'll show up on Google Maps and in search results. Sometimes, Google may require you to upload a video of your office and its surrounding areas.

Pro Tip: Add photos, logos, and a concise description with relevant keywords. This boosts Credibility and helps lenders, vendors, and customers find you.

Bing Places for Business

Go to bingplaces.com.

Duplicate the same info from your Google Business Profile.

Yelp for Business

Go to biz.yelp.com.

Yelp is not just for restaurants; lenders and vendors also check it as part of their business verification process.

Better Business Bureau (BBB) (Optional, but powerful)

Listing with the BBB adds Credibility. Lenders respect it, but note there's usually a fee ($30–$100/month, depending on your region).

Business Directories

At a minimum, list your business on these:

Manta.com

MerchantCircle.com

Superpages.com

Local.com

Step 2: Social Media Business Profiles

Even if you're not active on social media, lenders still expect your company to maintain a consistent and professional presence across major platforms. Create business accounts with the same name, phone number, website, and logo:

Facebook Business Page

Instagram Business Profile

LinkedIn Company Page

X (formerly Twitter) Business Account

Pro Tip: Consistently use the same branding (logo, colors, description) across all platforms. This consistency builds trust.

Step 3: Record Everything

After setting up your listings, create a master log that includes:

Sites where your business is listed

Your usernames and passwords

The exact business info you used

Pro Tip: *If you move offices, change your phone number, or update your website,* make sure to update your information everywhere. Otherwise, lenders may find conflicting details and reject your application.

The Key Rule: Consistency = Credibility

Remember this: The best product doesn't always win. The most recognized one does.

Your online presence is how lenders, vendors, and customers "see" you before they ever meet you. The stronger and more consistent your presence, the more credible and fundable your business becomes.

Review (Where We Are So Far)

By now, you should have:

- LLC documents in hand
- An Operating Agreement
- Your EIN secured
- A professional business email
- A domain and website
- A virtual office address
- A dedicated business phone number
- A logo and branding
- Your website is live
- Business listings online across major platforms

You're no longer just a hustler; you're running an official business that appears credible to lenders, vendors, and clients.

CHAPTER 5

BUSINESS CREDIT BUREAUS

"Rule number one: Don't lose money. Rule number two: Don't forget rule number one." — Warren Buffett

We've been focused on building your business credit, not your personal credit. But let me be honest with you, if your personal credit score is below 700, you should still work on improving it. A strong personal credit file can open doors, especially when you're just starting and lenders require a personal guarantee.

That said, business credit operates in its own world. It allows your company to stand independently, without relying on your Social Security number.

Personal Credit vs. Business Credit

Personal Credit: Reported by Experian, Equifax, and TransUnion.

Your personal credit score is a FICO score ranging from 300 to 850. You can check all three reports for free once a year at annualcreditreport.com.

Business Credit: Reported by Dun & Bradstreet (DNB), Experian Business, Equifax Business, and the Small Business Financial Exchange (SBFE).

Business credit is tracked differently, using scores like:

- **Paydex Score (DNB):** Ranges from 0 to 100. A score above 80 means your business pays on time.

- **Intelliscore (Experian):** Ranges from 1 to 100. A higher score indicates lower risk.

- **Business Delinquency Score (Equifax):** Predicts the likelihood of missed payments.

With the SBFE, only banks can report to them, so you really don't have anything to worry about.

Pro Tip: Lenders *often* check multiple credit bureaus, so it's essential to build credit with all three.

The Big 3 Business Credit Bureaus

1. Dun & Bradstreet (DNB)

DNB is the leader in business credit. Most vendors, banks, and leasing companies check it.

To get started, you need a D-U-N-S Number, which serves as your business's unique identifier in DNB's system.

You can apply for free at dnb.com.

Your Paydex Score is primarily based on your payment history. To obtain a score, you'll need at least three to five trade accounts reporting.

DNB also assigns a rating based on business size, time in business, and whether you've submitted financials.

Pro Tip: Avoid spending money on DNB's paid "Credit Builder" programs. You can build your score naturally through vendors that report to the credit bureaus.

2. Experian Business

Experian's Intelliscore Plus ranges from 1 to 100 and predicts the likelihood of your business defaulting on its obligations.

You can't self-report accounts. The only way to build Experian is by doing business with vendors, banks, or credit card companies that report to Experian.

Many business credit cards and lenders report to Experian, making it one of the most widely used credit bureaus.

Pro Tip: Experian updates more frequently than DNB. Even a single small vendor tradeline can help you begin building credit here.

3. Equifax Business

Equifax tracks business payment history, bankruptcies, and public records.

Like Experian, you can't self-report accounts.

Banks and leasing companies often report to Equifax.

They use scores, such as the Business Delinquency Score, to measure payment risk.

Pro Tip: *Many small business owners are unaware that* they already have an Equifax Business profile until a lender checks it. Get ahead by monitoring your profile early.

How to Get Your D-U-N-S® Number (Step by Step)

Go to dnb.com and click Get a D-U-N-S Number.

Enter your business name and location. If your business isn't listed, select Get a D-U-N-S Number.

Complete your profile:

Use your full legal business name exactly as it appears on your LLC paperwork.

Use your business phone and email (not personal Gmail/Yahoo).

Use your virtual office or business address (not your home address).

DNB may try to upsell you with paid services. Skip those offers and select the free option.

Verification typically takes 15–30 days, but may be completed sooner.

Pro Tip: *If you need your D-U-N-S Number* quickly, you can opt for expedited processing by paying a fee. However, if you're patient, the free option works just as well.

Understanding Business Credit Scores

Paydex Score (DNB): 80+ = excellent (pays on time or early).

Experian Intelliscore: Above 76 = low risk.

Equifax Business Scores: Higher scores mean lower risk to lenders.

Most lenders want to see:

DNB Paydex of 80 or higher
Experian Intelliscore of 76 or higher
No late payments, bankruptcies, or negative records

Why This Matters

When you apply for credit, lenders don't just look at your application; they look at your business credit reports. A strong profile means:

- Higher credit limits
- Lower interest rates
- Faster approvals
- Less need for a personal guarantee

Without established business credit, you'll always rely on your personal credit and Social Security number for funding.

CHAPTER 6

BUSINESS BANK ACCOUNTS

"Whatever you are thinking, think bigger."

— Tony Hsieh

We've handled the paperwork; now it's time to handle the money.

This chapter is all about where your money lives: the banks. Opening a business bank account isn't optional; it's essential. You'll want at least two accounts:

- A business account with a national bank

- A business account with a credit union

- Why both? Because they serve different purposes.

National Banks

Examples: Chase (JP Morgan), Wells Fargo, Bank of America, PNC Bank, Truist, U.S. Bank

Why they matter: They're recognized nationwide and internationally.
They can lend larger sums once your business profile is established.

They have advanced online banking and integrations.

Downside: National banks can be strict with new businesses. Without established credit or revenue history, approvals may take longer.

Credit Unions

Examples: Navy Federal Credit Union (NFCU), DCU, Penfed Credit Union

Local community credit unions

Why they matter: They're member-owned and often more flexible with small businesses.

- They often approve loans faster than big banks.

- They usually offer lower interest rates.

Pro Tip: With credit unions, you can often sit down with decision-makers directly, something you'll rarely do at a mega-bank.

Why You Need Both

Your business banking history will be checked when you apply for credit. Lenders want to see:

How long have you had your accounts open
How much money flows through them
Whether you maintain good balances

The longer your banking history, the stronger your approval odds.

Business Bank Account Requirements

Before you walk into the bank, have these ready:

1. Certificate of Formation (from Secretary of State)

2. IRS EIN Letter

3. Operating Agreement

4. Driver's License or Passport

5. Second form of ID (credit or debit card)

6. Proof of address (utility bill, lease, etc.)

Secured Business Credit Cards

If your personal FICO is below 700, don't worry — you can still build business credit by using secured business credit cards.

How it works:

You deposit money with the bank (typically a minimum of $500).

Your deposit becomes your credit limit.

You use the card for business expenses and pay it off in full each month.

After 6–12 months of on-time payments, banks may graduate you to an unsecured card and refund your deposit.

Examples of banks offering secured business credit cards:

Wells Fargo

Bank of America

BBVA (PNC)

First National Bank

Pro Tip: The more banks reporting your secured cards, the faster your business credit profile will grow.

Credit Unions and Builder Programs

Many credit unions offer special credit builder loans or small secured cards designed to help businesses establish credit.

Example: Navy Federal Credit Union (NFCU) often requires a military connection for membership. However, if someone in your network is a member, they can invite you to join.

Action Step: Search for a local credit union in your city. Call and ask:

Do you offer business accounts?

Do you offer secured business credit cards or builder loans?

What documents are required to join?

Key Rules for Banking Success

Always separate personal and business finances; never use your personal account for business expenses.

Stay consistent. Use the same business name, address, phone, and email as on your EIN, LLC docs, and online listings.

Maintain a good history. Lenders will review your bank account's age, balances, and transaction history.

Use your cards wisely. Pay off secured cards early and in full to improve your Paydex and Intelliscore ratings.

CHAPTER 7

STARTER VENDOR ACCOUNTS

"Learn the art of patience. Apply discipline to your thoughts when they become anxious over the outcome of a goal. Impatience breeds anxiety, fear, discouragement, and failure. Patience creates confidence, decisiveness, and a rational outlook, which eventually leads to Success!"

— *Brian Adams*

Why Vendor Accounts Matter

On your business credit report, every account that reports is called a *tradeline*. The easiest way to establish tradelines is through Net 30 vendor accounts.

A Net 30 account allows you to order supplies or services now and pay within 30 days. When you pay on time, the vendor reports your positive payment history to the credit bureaus.

This is the foundation of building business credit.

Especially useful if your personal credit score is below 700 and you need business credit to establish independence.

How Vendor Accounts Work

Vendors supply your business with products or services.

You place an order (usually $50 or more).

The vendor approves you for Net 30 terms.

You pay your invoice within 30 days.

The vendor reports your payment to DNB, Experian, or Equifax.

Over time, these accounts build your Paydex score and open the door to larger credit lines, fleet cards, and bank loans.

Tier System for Business Credit

Vendors and lenders are grouped into Tiers.

- **Tier 1**: Starter vendors (easy approval, no personal credit check).

- **Tier 2**: Larger vendors with Net 30 + revolving accounts.

- **Tier 3**: Retail accounts (Office Depot, Staples, Best Buy, etc.).

- **Tier 4**: Big retailers and fleet accounts (Amazon, Costco, Shell, etc.).

- **Tier 5**: Business credit cards and higher-limit revolving accounts.

You'll begin at Tier 1 and move upward as your credit file grows.

Tier 1 Vendors (Starter Accounts – 2025 Updated List)

Start with 3–5 of these. Pay on time for at least 3–6 months.

Quill – Office supplies, $50 minimum order. Reports to DNB.

www.quill.com

Summa Office Supplies: Digital products, with a minimum purchase of $60. Reports to Equifax & Experian.

www.summaofficesupplies.com

Crown Office Supplies: Reports to all three bureaus. Often requires a small membership fee.

www.crownofficesupplies.com

Uline: Shipping/warehouse supplies. Reports to DNB.

www.uline.com

Grainger: Industrial and safety supplies. Reports to DNB.

www.grainger.com

Shirtsy: Custom apparel. Reports to DNB, Experian, and Equifax.

www.shirtsy.com

Nav Business Boost: Credit monitoring + tradeline. $39.99/mo subscription. Reports to all 3.

www.nav.com

Creative Analytics: Digital marketing services. Reports to Equifax & Experian.

Pro Tip: Always ship to your business address (not your home), and ensure your profile details match your EIN, LLC, and DNB file.

How to Use Tier 1 Accounts

- Place your first order ($50–$100).

- At checkout, select Net 30 Terms (or call to request this option).

- Pay the invoice early (not just on time).

- Repeat for 3–6 months.

- Check that the vendors are reporting.

After 3–6 months, you should have the following:

- 3–5 vendor tradelines reporting

- Paydex score around 80

- Foundation to move into Tier 2

Tier 2 Vendors (Next Level)

These vendors offer stronger credit lines and some revolving accounts. Apply after you have 3–5 Tier 1 accounts reporting.

Examples:

- Reliable Office Supplies

- Aramark Work Apparel

- Tech Depot

- Global Industrial

- Home Depot Commercial Account

These vendors may report to DNB, Experian, and Equifax. You should aim for 5–10 tradelines total before moving on.

Tier 3: Retail Accounts

These are store credit lines at major retailers. Usually require:

- Paydex 70+

- 6+ months of history

- 5–10 tradelines reporting

Examples:

- Office Depot

- Staples

- Best Buy

- Conoco (fuel card)

- BP / Shell / Texaco

Tier 4: Large Retailers & Fleet Accounts

At this point, congratulations, you'll have 11–18 tradelines and strong scores. Now you can apply for accounts with:

- Dell

- Amazon Business

- Apple Business

- Costco

- ExxonMobil / Wright Express

These accounts typically offer higher credit limits, ranging from $5,000 to $50,000.

Tier 5: Business Credit Cards

After establishing a solid reporting history, you can apply for actual business credit cards that don't require a personal guarantee.

Examples:

- Key Bank Business Card

- Global Fleet MasterCard

- Fleet Cards USA

Lenders will pull credit reports from DNB, Experian, and Equifax.

Key Rules for Success

- Always use your business information (never personal).

- Pay invoices early and in full.

- Keep accounts active by placing at least one order every 90 days.

- Track your progress using Nav or directly from bureaus.

CHAPTER 8

BUSINESS CREDIT CARDS

"Whatever the mind can conceive and believe, it can achieve."

— Napoleon Hill

When to Apply for Business Credit Cards

Only move into this step when:

You've completed the earlier tiers (vendor and retail accounts).

You have at least 5–10 tradelines reporting to one of the major credit bureaus, such as DNB, Experian, or Equifax.

Your Paydex score is between 75 and 80 or higher.

Ideally, you also have a personal FICO score of 700 or above for PG cards.

Business credit cards are powerful tools, but applying too early can hurt your approval chances.

Banks That Offer Strong Business Credit Cards (2025)

- **Capital One:** Spark Business Cards (excellent starter PG card).

- **Bank of America:** Cash Rewards & Unlimited Cash Back Business.

- **Chase:** Ink Business Preferred, Ink Business Cash.

- **American Express (Amex):** Blue Business Plus, Amex Business Gold.

- **PNC Bank:** Business Options and Business Cash.

- **Wells Fargo:** Business Platinum & Secured Business Credit.

- **Navy Federal Credit Union**: Great for members with military ties.

Amex has become one of the most powerful issuers for small businesses, offering high limits and cards that scale with your revenue growth.

How Banks Check Your Business

Banks use credit bureaus to pull your business and/or personal credit when you apply.

- **Experian Business:** Pulled by Amex, Capital One, Citi.

- **Equifax Business:** Pulled by Bank of America, PNC.

- **Dun & Bradstreet (DNB):** Used by fleet and vendor cards.

- **TransUnion (personal):** Some issuers may check this if you use a PG.

Pro Tip: *Before applying, research which bureau each* bank uses. *Check forums like my FICO or Credit Boards for current data.*

Application Strategy

When you apply:

Group applications and inquiries are directed to the same bureau simultaneously.

Example: Apply for 2–3 cards that pull Experian on the same day.

The next day, apply for 2–3 cards that pull from Equifax.

Next, apply for those who pull TransUnion.

Apply for 6–9 business credit cards total. Typical limits range from $10,000 to $50,000 each.

Use the same business information everywhere (EIN, LLC, address, DNB profile).

Using Your Business Credit Cards Wisely

Always pay balances before the due date. Consistent, on-time payments for 3–6 months are essential.

Keep utilization under 30 percent (ideally below 10 percent).

Use the cards strictly for business expenses.

After 3–6 months, these cards should be reported to Experian and Equifax, which will boost your Paydex and Intelliscore.

Transaction Building Strategy

Use your cards for legitimate business expenses such as ads, inventory, and supplies.

Pay vendors that accept credit cards.

Use services like Plastiq or MelioPay to pay bills that typically don't accept credit cards.

This way, you still build a strong transaction history without red flags.

Revenue Alignment

When applying, banks will often ask about annual business revenue. Remember, this is what you anticipate making in your first year.

Be realistic yet optimistic. For early-stage businesses, reporting revenue of $100,000–$250,000 is common. For more mature companies, align with what you're actually depositing into your business bank account.

Key Rules for Business Credit Card Success

Don't submit random applications; be strategic.

Separate business and personal spending.

Build 3–6 months of history before trying to increase limits.

Track your reports regularly (use Nav or direct bureau pulls).

Remember, your credit limits and approvals will grow in tandem with your banking history, revenue, and credit tradelines. Often, for new businesses, you will have to guarantee personally.

CHAPTER 9

BUSINESS LINES OF CREDIT (LOC)

"The borrower is servant to the lender."

— Proverbs 22:7

What is a Business Line of Credit?

A Line of Credit (LOC) is a flexible financing option that allows your business to borrow funds as needed, up to a predetermined limit. Unlike a traditional loan, where you receive one lump sum, you only pay interest on the amount you actually use.

Typical approval ranges from 8% to 10% of your annual revenue.

Funds are placed in an account that you can access at any time.

It's ideal for managing cash flow, payroll, and working capital.

How to Position Yourself for Approval

Banks typically look for:

- Consistent monthly deposits into your business account.

- At least 6–12 months of operating history.

- Solid business credit profile (Paydex score 75+, multiple trade lines).

Example: If your business deposits around $50,000 per month (about $600,000 annually), the bank may approve you for a $48,000 to $60,000 line of credit.

Start with a smaller amount (for example, a $25,000 to $30,000 line of credit) to establish repayment history, then request increases over time.

Best Banks for Business LOCs (2025)

- Chase Business Line of Credit

- Bank of America Business Advantage LOC

- Capital One LOC

- PNC Bank Business LOC

- Wells Fargo Prime Line of Credit

Common Questions Banks May Ask

1. What does your business do?

Please keep it simple, focused, and growth-oriented.

Example: "We provide logistics and supply chain solutions to small businesses."

2. How long have you been in business?

Answer consistently with your DNB and Secretary of State filings.

3. What is the purpose of the line of credit?

Always answer clearly: *Working capital to grow the business.*

4. What is your gross/net profit?

Be prepared to present deposits that support your revenue claims.

5. Do you own property? What is your personal income?

These questions may arise if you're applying with a personal guarantor.

Pro Tip for LOC Success: *Maintain consistent deposits. Banks love predictability.*

Avoid overdrafts; even one can reduce your chances of approval.

Request credit limit increases every six to twelve months after establishing a good repayment record.

CHAPTER 10

LEASING A COMPANY VEHICLE

"If people aren't calling you crazy, you're not thinking big enough."

— Richard Branson

Why Lease Through Your Business?

Leasing a vehicle through your business helps you build a strong credit history with auto lenders.

It also offers tax advantages, as lease payments can be deducted as business expenses.

Additionally, it offers liability protection because the vehicle is registered in your company's name rather than your own.

When registered under your LLC:

The license plates and title reflect your business name and address.

Your privacy is protected if someone runs your plate number information.

How to Lease Your First Vehicle

Focus on leasing a new vehicle instead of a used one, as banks consider new cars a lower risk.

Keep your first lease under $50,000.

Ensure your Paydex score is 75–80 or higher, with several established tradelines.

When applying, look for manufacturers that offer corporate leasing programs, such as Toyota, Ford, GM, BMW, Mercedes-Benz, and Honda.

Lease vs. Purchase

Lease: Lower upfront cost, flexibility, and the option to upgrade every 2–3 years.

Purchase: Higher long-term commitment, more capital tied up, and eventual depreciation.

For your first company vehicle, leasing is often the more intelligent choice to reduce financial exposure and maintain flexibility.

Tax Benefits

Lease payments can generally be deducted as business expenses.

Insurance and maintenance costs may also be eligible for write-offs.

Consult a certified public accountant (CPA) to explore potential deductions under Section 179 or mileage-based write-offs.

CHAPTER 11

CORPORATE LEASE A PROPERTY

"It's the little details that are vital. Little things make big things happen."

— John Wooden

What is a Corporate Lease?

A corporate lease occurs when your business leases property, such as an apartment, house, office, or townhome, under the company's name instead of your personal name.

This is common for relocating employees or providing executive housing.
Corporate leases can also be used for company-owned housing or business operations.

The lease is tied to your business credit profile, not your personal credit.

Advantages of Corporate Leasing

- Builds your business credit history beyond vendors and credit cards.

- Provides privacy (the lease shows the company, not your personal name).

- Increases approval odds, since landlords often prefer companies over individuals.

- Can be structured through LLCs to separate liability and protect assets.

How to Apply for a Corporate Lease

- Contact the property owner or management company.

- Inform them that you are applying for a corporate lease.

Provide:

- Business credit references.

- Bank statements or trade references.

- Business credit report (DNB or Experian)

Asset Protection Strategy with LLCs

- Many investors use separate LLCs for each property, vehicle, or asset.

- Keeps liabilities isolated.

- Protects your leading operating company.

Example: A truck might be owned by "New Truck LLC," while rental properties are under separate LLCs.

Pro Tip: Corporate leases are also an alternative path if your personal credit has challenges or a history. Approval is based on your company's credit, revenue, and banking history, not your personal score.

CHAPTER 12

ASSET PROTECTION AND PRIVACY

"You have the potential to influence many people's lives positively greatly. And if you don't realize that potential, then you're being somewhat selfish because you're not giving to others and helping them achieve their financial goals. Which, by the way, will help you reach yours too (and then some)."

— *Joe Fairless*

Why Asset Protection Matters

Asset protection and privacy are more important than ever. Lawsuits, creditors, and even competitors can threaten everything you've worked so hard to build. To safeguard yourself and your business, it is essential to structure ownership in a way that protects your assets and preserves your privacy.

Several strategies can help achieve this. In this book, we will focus primarily on the LLC (Limited Liability Company), which remains one of the most effective tools for entrepreneurs and investors.

Always consult an experienced asset protection attorney before finalizing your structure.

The Power of the LLC

- An LLC is a separate legal entity from its owners. This separation means:

- The owners (members) are not personally liable for the LLC's debts or lawsuits.

- Assets owned by the LLC are generally protected from personal liability.

Almost any asset property, vehicles, equipment, or intellectual property can be owned by an LLC.
Major companies and wealthy individuals use LLCs to separate and protect their assets. By placing your investments under LLCs, you add a critical layer of protection.

Avoid Piercing the Corporate Veil

The corporate veil separates your personal life from your business life. When maintained properly, it keeps you protected. However, if you mix personal and business finances, a court can 'pierce the veil' and hold you personally liable.

Common mistakes that can pierce the corporate veil include:

- Using business accounts for personal expenses.

- Failing to maintain proper records or operating agreements

Committing fraud in the business

Tip: Never mix personal and business funds. Keep business bank accounts, credit cards, and accounting completely separate. This not only protects you legally but also strengthens your business credit profile.

Why Some States Are Better Than Others

Not all states treat LLCs the same. For example, in Texas, whether the corporate veil can be pierced is often left to the discretion of the judge. Other states, such as Delaware, Nevada, and Wyoming, have stronger LLC protections built into law.

Many entrepreneurs choose to form their LLCs in these states (especially Wyoming) because they offer:

Strong privacy (owners' names aren't publicly listed).

Low annual fees.

Robust asset protection laws.

Advanced Strategy: Offshore Trusts & LLCs

For ultimate protection, some high-net-worth individuals establish offshore trusts in conjunction with LLCs. For example:

A trust in the Cook Islands may hold a Nevis LLC.

A Cook Islands trustee manages the trust, meaning U.S. courts cannot force them to return assets.

This provides powerful protection, but it's costly and not necessary for most small businesses. Still, it's worth knowing as your wealth grows.

Practical Steps You Can Take Today

Form Separate LLCs for Each Asset

For example, one LLC for each rental property, one for your trucking business, and another for your intellectual property.

This keeps liabilities isolated: if one gets sued, the others are protected.

Use Business Credit Strategically

Build strong credit for each LLC. Over time, each can qualify for its own business lines of credit, loans, and vendor accounts.

This multiplies your access to funding.

Privacy Matters

Consider using a registered agent service instead of listing your personal name and address on your documents.

This keeps your personal details off public records.

Creating Capital LLC – Our Approach

At my company, Creating Capital LLC, we believe asset protection is just as important as asset growth. That's why we structure deals and investments using multiple entities and layers of protection. By combining LLCs, credit-building strategies, and privacy measures, we minimize risk while maximizing opportunity.

The goal is simple: Grow wealth, protect assets, and maintain privacy.

CLOSING

I hope you've gained a wealth of valuable information throughout this book. My challenge to you is simple: keep learning, keep building, and keep applying what you've learned. Business credit, funding, and wealth-building are not one-time events; they are lifelong skills that require ongoing development and maintenance. The financial landscape is constantly evolving, and those who adapt will continue to thrive.

At Creating Capital LLC, our mission is to help entrepreneurs and investors like you succeed. We invest in high-quality assets across real estate, entertainment, and private equity, partnering with individuals who are ready to take their businesses to the next level. Whether it is hard money lending for real estate or partnerships in larger projects, we believe in building strong, profitable relationships that benefit everyone involved.

Beyond deals and investments, we are building a movement.

Creating Capital Community

The Creating Capital Community is our membership platform designed for people who want to learn and grow in real estate, business credit, and wealth-building strategies. Through live weekly sessions, resources, and group coaching, we provide the tools and support you need to turn knowledge into action. Whether you are starting with your first LLC, jumping into real estate investing, or looking to scale into multifamily developments, this community guides you step by step.

Personal Mentorship with Lee Price III

For those who are truly serious about accelerating their growth, I also offer personal mentorship programs. This is where I work directly with you to create a customized blueprint for your business and investments. My mentorship is designed to help you:

- Build and structure business credit the right way.

- Secure funding and leverage it for real estate deals.

- Scale from single-family projects into multifamily and commercial investments.

- Develop the wealth-building mindset needed to create lasting Success.

- Mentorship with me is not just about information; it's about transformation.

Business Credit Building Services

I know this book provided you with a wealth of information. And let's be honest, if you're feeling a little overwhelmed, that's completely normal. Building business credit the right way takes time, patience, and discipline.

But here's the good news: you don't have to do it alone.

At Creating Capital LLC, we offer done-for-you services where my team and I will:

- Structure and set up your business entity properly
- Build out your complete business profile so it's lender-ready
- Establish and manage your business credit accounts step by step
- Position you for funding so you can focus on running and growing your business

If you'd rather have experts take the wheel while you focus on your vision, we can build out your business credit for you completely.

Your Next Step

If you've found value in these pages and are ready to take action, I invite you to join our movement.

Visit www.CreatingCapitalHTX.com/community to learn more about:

- Joining the Creating Capital Community

- Applying for my personal mentorship programs.

- Exploring partnership opportunities with Creating Capital LLC

Remember, opportunities are everywhere, but they only matter if you act on them. Your journey to building business credit, accessing capital, and creating generational wealth starts with the decision to take the next step.

Let's build together.

Lee Price III

Founder & CEO, Creating Capital LLC

www.ingramcontent.com/pod-product-compliance
Lightning Source LLC
Chambersburg PA
CBHW040908210326
41597CB00029B/5014